MIX AND MATCH

Activities for Classification

BY RUTH WHITE
and MARILYN REHWALD

Illustrations by CARY MESHUL

RHYTHMS PRODUCTIONS
Los Angeles, California 90034

Would you mix or match
Your shoes and socks?

Would you mix or match
Your keys with locks?

Would you mix or match
Forks and knives?

Would you mix or match
Bees and hives?

Would you mix or match
A nickle and a quarter?

Do you mix or match
To put things in order?

MIX AND MATCH
Activities for Classification

RHYTHMS PRODUCTIONS, Los Angeles, California 90034-0485

ISBN 0-934042-01-2

INTRODUCTION

We put things in order by arranging them in some way or by creating categories. This process is called classification.

Young children use their senses to sort by color, size or shape. At the beginning level, children perceive things as they seem to be. Apples may be red or green; pencils, long or short, etc.

Gradually, as thinking develops beyond the purely perceptual level, things may be classified by other than appearance. The child begins to use intellect or reasoning to classify and may organize objects by their function. For instance, in a group of objects, a child may find things that are used for travel (vehicles) or eating (utensils).

The methods by which children classify also alter with their developmental levels. At first, young people organize things according to the ideas that are given to them. As they develop a capacity for independent thinking, they are able to arrange things using their own ideas. For instance, in the beginning, a child is directed or told how to sort the objects (by color, etc.). Later, the child sorts objects and tells how he or she did so (by color, etc.).

It should be emphasized that classification concepts cannot be taught at an intellectual level. They must be learned through activities and very often, through trial and error. The purpose of this book is to suggest activities for acquiring classification skills.

The objectives of the book are:

1. For children to understand the importance of classification.

2. For children to master classification skills at six developmental levels.

3. For children to apply classification skills independently to everyday living.

TABLE OF CONTENTS

PART I

Developmental Activities for Classification

LEVEL 1

IDENTIFYING OBJECTS BY ONE DESCRIPTIVE CHARACTERISTIC

Children first learn to recognize color, then shape and finally size as characteristics (attributes) for classification.

At this level, the teacher or an adult helps the child by suggesting the classification categories. Level 1 games and activities are most effective when done on a one-to-one basis (adult-child) or in small groups of not more than six.

SORTING SHAPES

Objective   *To sort by shape or color*

Preparation   *Color and cut one copy of worksheet 1. Spread shapes in front of child (or small group)*

Show me all of the red shapes.

Show me all of the yellow shapes.

Show me all of the blue shapes.

Show me all of the green shapes.

Show me all of the circles.

Show me all of the triangles.

Show me all of the squares.

Show me all of the diamonds.

Find the shapes that are alike in some way and put them here (point).

How are they alike?

8

NECKLACES

Objective   *To string beads by color and shape.*

Preparation *Give each child a string or shoe lace and beads in two colors and two shapes.*

Make a necklace of all the red beads.

How are the beads alike?

Find all the beads that are alike in some other way and string them together to make a necklace.

How are the beads alike?

Can you make another necklace using beads that are alike in some way?

Draw a picture of the necklace you made.

SORT A PERSON

Objective   *To match shapes.*

Preparation *Use a large circle (or 10-inch paper plate), a large square (or dinner napkin), a large triangle (or folded napkin) and a large diamond (construction paper).*

Cut shapes from worksheets 3 and 4. Sort them in a muffin tin.

Place the paper plate (or circle) and muffin tin in front of child. Have other large shapes nearby for child to use later.

Make a "Round Person" as child (or small group) watches.

This is "Round Person." Why do you suppose this is "Round Person?"

Pick up a triangle and use it for a nose here (point).

Is this still "Round Person?" Why not?

Make this be "Round Person" again.

What would "Square Person" look like?

What would "Triangle Person" look like?

What would "Diamond Person" look like?

Make a "Mixed-up Person."

SHAPE PERSON

Objective   *To sort by shape and create a "shape person."*

Preparation   *Set up "Shape Person" art activity for children to work on during free time.*

Provide large construction paper shapes in various colors. Cut worksheets 3 and 4 and sort in muffin tins; or provide dittoed shapes for children to cut.

Have children create "shape person" by gluing small shapes on large shape. Display "Shape People" on bulletin boards.

Have children tell a story about their "Shape Person."

Make your favorite "Shape Person." Tell me a story about your "Shape Person."

11

BIG AND LITTLE MATCH GAME

Objective   *To sort objects by size.*

Preparation   *Use six pairs of objects that are alike except for size. Possible objects include large and small salt containers, tablespoon and teaspoon, large and small cereal boxes, large and small glass, large and small frozen juice cans, large and small cans of same brand foodstuffs.*

Place objects at random in front of child and have the child match objects which are alike.

Emphasize proper size terminology: bigger than, smaller than.

Find the objects that look alike and put them together.

How are they alike?

How are they different?

OTHER GAMES AND ACTIVITES FOR LEVEL 1

The following games and activites from Part II can be used with this level:

BEAD GAME #1

GATHERING STONES

NATURE WALK

CARS

TV TIME

MISCELLANEOUS CLASSIFICATION IDEAS

FLYING

MURALS

PRACTICAL APPLICATION: DAILY LIVING

PRACTICAL APPLICATION: SCHOOL

PRACTICAL APPLICATION: LIBRARY

WHERE TO FIND IT

PEOPLE, PLACES, THINGS

PICK AND SORT

CONCENTRATION

SOURPUSS

WHAT COLOR?

THE MARKET

LEVEL 2

IDENTIFYING OBJECTS BY MORE THAN ONE DESCRIPTIVE CHARACTERISTIC

An object may be classified by more than one characteristic. For instance, by size and shape (big, square), color and shape (red square) or size and color (small, blue ball).

By asking such questions as "Would this work just as well? Why? Why Not?", the teacher can help guide the child into extended thinking.

Level 2 games and activities are most effective when done on a one-to-one basis (adult-child) or in small groups of not more than six.

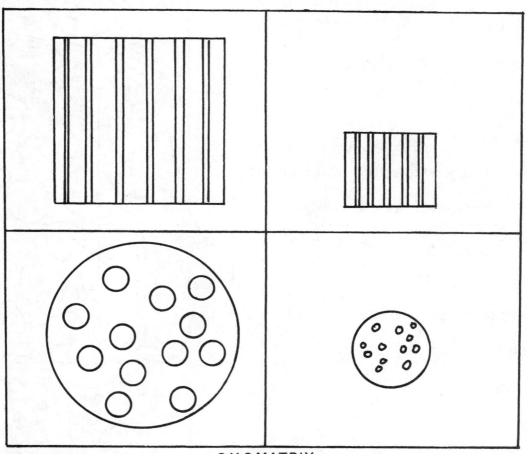

2 X 2 MATRIX

A matrix is a graph of information which shows a pattern of relationship between two objects. The matrix is used in this unit as an effective teaching tool for illustrating dual characteristics.

14

MATRIX GAME 1

Objective   *To show the relationship between object and color by sorting pictures on a matrix.*

Preparation   *Use worksheet 5 and worksheet 9, pictures A, B, C, D, E, and F. Color the pictures.*

A green	*D green*
B green	*E yellow*
C yellow	*F yellow*

Use pictures A, B, and C to set up the matrix as shown. Place the other picture cards at random in front of the child. Have child choose the right picture to complete matrix.

Look at the matrix (point). See the space that is empty? One of these cards (point to cards outside matrix) will finish the matrix. Which card do you think it is? Put it in the matrix.

Why did you choose that picture? Would this one work just as well? (Point to card not chosen.)

Would this one work (point to other card not chosen)? Why not?

15

MATRIX GAME 2

Objective   *To show the relationship between object, color and size by sorting pictures on a matrix.*

Preparation   *Use worksheet 6 and worksheet 9, pictures G, H, I, J, K, L, M, N, O, and P. Color the pictures.*

G green	K red	N red
H green	L red	O yellow
I yellow	M red	P yellow
J yellow		

Use pictures G, H, I, K to set up matrix as shown. Place the other six pictures at random in front of child. Have child choose right pictures to complete matrix.

Look at the matrix (point). See the spaces that are empty.

Now look at the turtles in the first row. Tell me how they are alike.

Tell me how they are different.

Look at the cup in the next row. Which picture goes in the empty space so this row matches the first row? Why did you choose that picture?

Choose the picture which goes here (point to empty space in third row) to finish the matrix.

Do all the rows match? How do you know?

SHAPE MATRIX

Objective   *To show relationship between shape and color by sorting on a matrix.*

Preparation   *Use worksheet 8. Color and cut worksheet 1. Place matrix and shapes in front of child.*

Set up matrix as shown. Have child or children choose the right shapes to complete the matrix. If this appears to be too difficult, add shapes— until child can complete task.

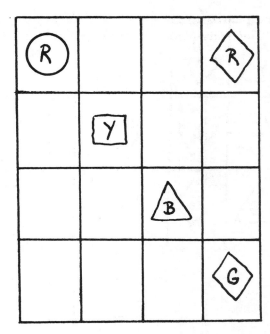

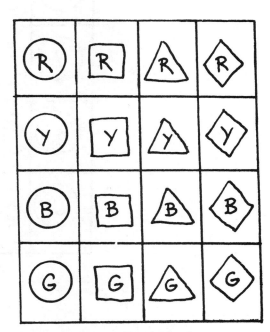

Completed Matrix.

Look at the matrix. See the empty spaces.

Finish the matrix by placing the shapes in the right place.

What is the same about the first row? (point horizontally)

What is the same about the second column? (point vertically)

Close your eyes while I do something to the matrix. (switch two shapes)

Open your eyes and tell me what is wrong.

Fix it so it looks right.

WHAT'S MISSING?

Objective   *To recognize relationships between shape and color.*

Preparation   *Use completed matrix from SHAPE MATRIX game. Place in front of small group of children.*

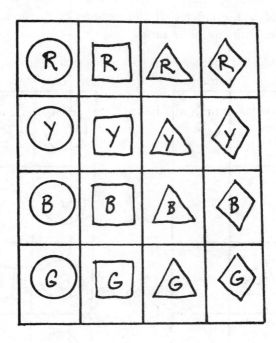

Have children close eyes while one child takes a shape off the matrix. The children open eyes to see what is missing. Children must name the missing piece by color and shape. The one who guesses right takes away the shape in the next game.

Vary the game by taking away two or three shapes.

Close your eyes while (child's name) takes a shape off the matrix.

Open your eyes. Guess what is missing.

18

THE THREE BEARS

Objective: *To show the relationship of size and function by sorting pictures on a matrix.*

Preparation: *Read the story* The Three Bears. *Discuss sequence.*

               Use worksheet 10 and worksheet 7. Have children cut out the bears, bowls, chairs, and beds and glue them on the matrix by size and function.

Cut out the bears and glue them in the top row of the matrix. Try to glue the biggest bear in the first box and the smallest bear in the last box.

Now cut out the bowls, chairs, and beds. Can you match them to the right bear?

Color your picture.

BEAD GAME

Objective   *To use shape and color to verbally describe beads.*

Preparation   *Seat two children so they are hidden from each other by a screen (or back-to-back). Use two laces and two identical sets of beads. Each set contains 12 beads of any three colors and two shapes (For example: 3 cubes: one each in red, yellow, blue. 9 rounds: three each in red, yellow, blue).*

Give each child a set of beads and a lace. Choose one child to be the leader. The leader chooses a bead, strings the bead on a lace and describes it. The other child must find a matching bead and string it on a lace.

After stringing six beads, children compare necklaces. If necklaces don't match, start a new game. Repeated mismatches will require supervision.

Vary the game later by adding more beads to the sets or by having children take turns naming beads for the necklace.

Do you think that (child's name) can make a necklace just like yours without seeing your necklace?

Choose a bead to string on your necklace. Describe it to (child's name). (Child's name) will find the bead in the box and string it on a necklace.

After you both have six beads on your necklaces, stop and see if the necklaces look alike. Will they look alike if you do a good telling job and a good listening job? Why?

OTHER GAMES AND ACTIVITES FOR LEVEL 2

The following games and activities from Part II can be used with this level:

BEAD GAME #2

CARS

MISCELLANEOUS CLASSIFICATION IDEAS

FLYING

PICK AND SORT

CONCENTRATION

SOURPUSS

THE MARKET

LEVEL 3

IDENTIFYING OBJECTS BY THE TERM "NOT"

A group of related objects can be subdivided into smaller groups. For instance, a group of squares can be divided into large squares and small squares.

At this level, the term "not" is used to describe one of the groups. Thus, one of the squares sub-groups would be called either big squares and NOT big squares, or little squares and NOT little squares.

Level 3 games and activities are most effective when done on a one-to-one basis (adult-child) or in very small groups of not more than six.

SHOW AND TELL

Objective
: *To choose a shape by a negative description of its attributes.*

Preparation
: *Use worksheets 1 and 2. Color as directed. Place set of shapes in front of child or small group of children.*

Have child respond to directions by choosing an appropriate shape. Teacher must ask for shape by describing its negative attributes.

Have child discuss why it was chosen.

Show me please something *not* large. Why did you choose this shape?

Show me please something *not* red. Why did you choose this shape?

Show me please something *not* a square. Why did you choose this shape?

THE "NOT" GAME 1

Objective   *To describe a geometric shape by its negative attributes.*

Preparation   *Use worksheets 1 and 2. Color as directed. Place shapes in front of small group of children.*

Choose one child to pick a shape. The child picks a shape. The teacher asks questions about the shape. The child answers the question by describing the shape using negative attributes. The teacher records descriptions as not red, not square, not big, etc. on chalkboard.

Choose a shape. Tell me something "not" about its color.

What else can you tell me "not" about its color?

Tell me as many "not" things as you can abouts its shape.

Tell me something "not" about its size.

24

THE "NOT" GAME 2

Objective   *To describe a geometric shape by its negative attributes.*

Preparation   *Allow child to choose any shape of any color. Worksheet 1, 3, or 4 may be used. Or cut shape out of construction paper. Glue shape on a larger sheet of paper.*

Have children write descriptions of the shape using negative attributes.

Choose a shape you like and color it any color. Glue it on the big sheet of paper.

Write about the shape using the word *not*.

GUESS MY SHAPE

Objective   *To describe a geometric shape by its negative attributes.*

Preparation   *Use worksheet 1. Color as directed. Place shapes in a box. Choose one child to be "IT."*

IT picks a shape out of the box and hides it while group closes eyes. Group opens eyes and asks questions to guess the color and shape of the piece chosen. Answers to guesses are recorded on chalkboard. (For example, "Is This A Circle?" IT responds, "This is not a circle."

The first child to guess the color and shape of the missing piece is the new IT.

Vary the game by adding small shapes (worksheet 2) to the box.

Close your eyes while (child's name) takes a shape out of the box.

Now open your eyes and try to guess what is missing from the box.

Make good guesses. Read the clues before you make a guess.

DOGGIE DOGGIE

Objective   *To divide one group of objects into two subgroups and to describe one of the subgroups using the complement "not."*

Preparation   *Use worksheet 11. Cut pictures on the line and place in front of child. Discuss the variety of dogs in pictures.*

The game should be repeated several times until the child can sort the pictures and describe the subgroups without teacher prompting.

Divide the dogs into two groups. Put all of the collies in one group. Put the rest of the dogs in another group.

This is a group of collies (point).

Can you use the word *not* to describe this group of dogs? (not collies)

Use all of the dog pictures and divide them into two different groups. Remember to put only one kind of dog in one of the groups.

Name the dogs in this group (point to group containing one kind of dog).

What is the group not? (point to other group).

OTHER GAMES AND ACTIVITIES FOR LEVEL 3

The following games and activities from Part II can be used with this level:

BEAD GAME #3

CARS

MISCELLANEOUS CLASSIFICATION IDEAS

PERSON GAME

THE MARKET

LEVEL 4

QUANTATIVE COMPARISONS: "SOME" AND "ALL"

Within a group of related objects, part of the objects may have a unique characteristic. For instance, in a group of shapes, some of the shapes may be triangles.

At this level, the quantative terms "some" and "all" are used to make the comparisons between part of the group of objects and the whole group of objects. The teacher helps the child see that the objects of the smaller group ("some") Still belong to the whole group ("all").

Level 3 games and activities are most effective when done on a one-to-one basis (adult-child) or in very small groups of not more than six.

GOING TO THE ZOO

Objective   *To recognize that an object can belong to two groups simultaneously.*

Preparation   *Use worksheet 12. Cut zoo pictures on the line. Use box lid or yarn for zoo pen. Place pen in front of child. Hold animals until ready for use. Play often until child can respond without prompting.*

We're going to the zoo. What lives at the zoo? (animals)

How are elephants and bears alike? Are giraffes animals too?

What other animals might you see at the zoo?

Here are some zoo animals. (Place animals in front of child.) Put all of the bears in the pen.

Are there any animals left out of the pen? Are there more bears or more animals? Why? Are bears animals?

Put the bears back with the other animals. Now put all the animals in the pen. Are there any left out of the pen? Are there more animals or more bears? Can you tell me why?

SHAPE GAME

Objective   *To recognize that an object can have two attributes simultaneously.*

Preparation *Use worksheet 1 (colored as directed) and two lids. Place the lids and the shapes in front of the child.*

The game can be played repeatedly by changing the shape name or by changing to color as the attribute.

Vary the game by adding the small shapes (worksheet 2) to allow for sorting by size.

Play often until child can respond without prompting.

What shapes do you see?

Put all of the circles in one lid and all of the other shapes in the other lid.

Are some circles here? (Point to lid containing shapes not circles.) Are circles shapes? Are there more shapes or more circles? Why?

FLOWERS

Objective | *To recognize that an object can have two attributes simultaneously.*

Preparation | *Use worksheet 13. Color the tulips red and color the daisies yellow. Show child the field of flowers.*

Here is a field of flowers. What colors do you see? The yellow flowers are daisies (point) and the red flowers are tulips (point). Show me a daisy. Show me a tulip.

If I want to pick a very large bouquet of flowers, would I pick all the flowers or only the daisies?

If I pick the daisies, what would be left? Are tulips flowers too?

What would be more, all the flowers or a bunch of tulips?

What would be more, all the flowers or a bunch of daisies?

OTHER GAMES AND ACTIVITIES FOR LEVEL 4

The following games and activities from Part II can be used with this level:

BEAD GAME #4

CARS

MISCELLANEOUS CLASSIFICATION IDEAS

THE MARKET

LEVEL 5

IDENTIFYING OBJECTS BY ONE DESCRIPTIVE CHARACTERISTIC
(Advanced)

At level 5, the child finds a single characteristic to use in classifying a group of related objects. After sorting the objects, the child then describes the attribute used.

Classification at this level is similar to level 1. At level 1, an attribute for classification is given to the child, whereas at level 5, the attribute is discovered and described by the child. The primary role of the teacher is to give directions for the activity and to observe the performance of that activity.

Level 5 games and activities are most effective when done by the individual child or by two or three children working together.

CLASSIFY

Objective   *To sort cards into groups and define each group by its attribute.*

Preparation   *Use worksheets 14 and 15. Cut along lines.*
Give child cards.

Use all of the pictures and sort them in some way.

How did you sort the pictures? How are these pictures alike? (Point to foods.)

And these? (Point to vehicles.)

And these? (Point to animals.)

And these? (Point to tools.)

"JUNK"

Objective   *To sort objects into groups and define each group by its attribute.*

Preparation   *Have children collect "junk" for classifying. "Junk" must be relatively small in size. Coffee cans make good storage containers.*

Use sorting trays. Good containers for use as sorting trays include egg cartons, muffin tins, box lids, apple dividers, TV dinner trays.

Provide child with "junk" and sorting tray. Allow enough time to finish the sorting task.

This task can be repeated many times. The child can find several ways to classify.

Child may keep a record of the classification by drawing pictures of groups formed.

Accept any classification of "junk." A justifiable classification might be, "Stuff I like and stuff I don't like." Expand the child's thinking by asking if there is any other way to sort the "junk."

Sort the "junk" in some way.

Tell me about how you sorted this "junk."

OPTIONAL: When you finish, draw a picture to show how you sorted the "junk" or write a story that tells about how you sorted the "junk".

BUTTONS

Objective   *To sort buttons into groups and define each group by its attribute.*

Preparation   *Have children collect buttons.*

Give child a handful of about 12 buttons and a sorting tray.

Have child sort the buttons in some way.

The number of buttons can be increased as child gains proficiency with sorting or expresses an interest to work with larger numbers.

Several children can be sorting groups of buttons simultaneously.

Children may keep a record of the classification by making a simple drawing or a bar graph.

Sort the buttons in some way.

Tell me something about how you sorted the buttons.

OPTIONAL: Draw a picture to show how you sorted the buttons.

"SOMETHING" SPINNER GAME

Objective   *To name objects belonging to a class.*

Preparation *Use worksheet 16. Prepare spinner by cutting on lines and mounting on a piece of stiff paper or cardboard cut to the size of the spinner. Use a thin stick or a piece of cardboard cut in shape of arrow*
Punch a hole in arrow. Attach arrow to spinner with a paper brad. Use washers between spinner and arrow.

Place spinner in front of small group of children. Read words on spinner to children.

Have child spin the spinner and name an object which belongs to that group.

Spin the spinner. When the arrow lands on the space "vehicle" name a vehicle. What will you do when it lands on the "tool" space? On the "animal" space? On the "food" space? Do not name something that has already been named in this game.

OTHER GAMES AND ACTIVITIES FOR LEVEL 5

The following games and activities from Part II can be used with this level:

BEAD GAME #5

GATHERING STONES

NATURE WALK

CARS

WHAT SHALL I WEAR?

TV TIME

MISCELLANEOUS CLASSIFICATION IDEAS

FLYING

PRACTICAL APPLICATION: DAILY LIVING

PRACTICAL APPLICATION: SCHOOL

PRACTICAL APPLICATION: LIBRARY

WHERE TO FIND IT

PEOPLE, PLACES, THINGS

PICK AND SORT

CONCENTRATION

SOURPUSS

WHAT COLOR?

THE MARKET

LEVEL 6

IDENTIFYING OBJECTS BY MORE THAN ONE DESCRIPTIVE CHARACTERISTIC
(Advanced)

The child describes the attributes of more than one group of objects and realizes that an object can belong to more than one group at a time. The term *and* is used to describe the attributes of the object belonging to more than one group (blue and round)

Level 6 games and activities are most effective when done in small groups of from three to six children. The primary role of the teacher or adult at this level is to give directions for the activity and to observe the child's performance of that activity. Later two children may play some of the games independently.

Two overlapping circles (Venn diagram) is an effective tool to illustrate that an object can belong to two groups simultaneously. That object is placed in the intersection.

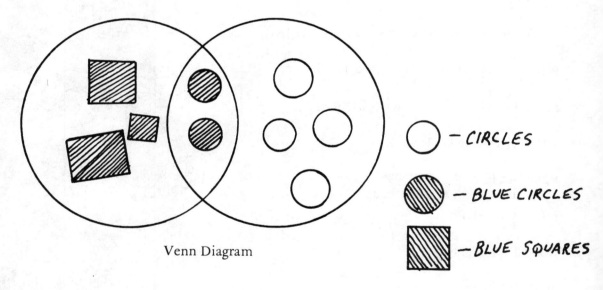

Venn Diagram

The intersection can only contain an object if the two groups are defined by two different attributes as color and shape, shape and size, color and size, but *not* color and color.

HOOP GAME #1

Objectives   *To show the relationship between two groups of objects by using two intersecting circles (Venn diagram).*

*To use the word **and** to describe the intersection of the two circles.*

Preparation   *Use two hula hoops. Place them on floor or ground in an overlapping position.*

Seat group of children around the hoops.

Some of the children will be used as objects to be placed in the hoops. Teacher chooses two attributes, keeping in mind the intersection. For example, hoop 1 might be all children wearing tennis shoes; hoop 2 might be all children wearing yellow. The intersection would contain all children wearing tennis shoes and wearing yellow.

Select children according to attributes chosen and place in correct position, i.e., hoop 1, hoop 2, or intersection. The rest of the group must guess or describe the common attributes of each hoop and the intersection.

Why are all these children in hoop 1? Find something the same about them that is different from the children in hoop 2.

How are the children in hoop 2 alike?

Are the children in the intersection (point) part of hoop 1? Are the children in the intersection (point) part of hoop 2?

How are the children in the intersection alike?

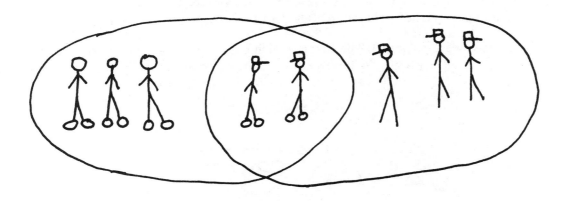

41

HOOP GAME #2.

Objectives   *To show the relationship between two groups of objects by using two intersecting circles (Venn diagram).*

*To use the word **and** to describe the attributes of the objects in the intersection of the two circles.*

Preparation   *Use worksheets 1 and 2. Color as directed. Cut out shapes and place on floor. Use two colors of yarn or plastic hoops. Place on floor to form two overlapping circles.*

Seat group of children around circles.

Teacher chooses two attributes as shape and size, shape and color, or color and size. Direct child to place all the shapes showing one of the attributes in one circle and to place all shapes showing the other attribute in the other circle. Guide children in group to see that some of the shapes in each circle have both attributes and must be placed in the intersection of the two circles.

Repeat game by changing combination of attributes. Play often.

Put all of the red shapes in hoop 1 (point).

Put all of the circles in hoop 2 (point).

Are all of the reds in hoop 1? (Point yes.) Are all of the circles in hoop 2? (Point no.)

Can you put all the circles in hoop 2? (Point.)

What color circle did you move? (Red.)

How are these shapes alike? (Point to hoop 1: red.)

How are these shapes alike? (Point to hoop 2: circles.)

Is there a shape that is red and a circle? (Yes.) Can you see a place to put it so it is part of the red group and part of the circle group? (Overlap.)

This is called the intersection (point). The shapes which go here belong to both groups. Do you see red and round shapes in the intersection?

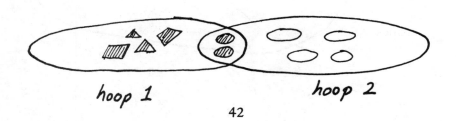

hoop 1   hoop 2

THE CITY GAME

Objectives
:   *To show the relationship between two groups of objects by using two intersecting circles (Venn diagram).*

    *To use the word **and** to describe the attributes of the objects in the intersection of the two circles.*

Preparation
:   *Use worksheets 1 and 2. Color as directed. Cut out shapes and place on floor. Use two colors of yarn or plastic hoops. Place on floor to form two overlapping circles.*

    Each circle represents a city. The teacher builds a city with some of the pieces from the shapes worksheets. Seat group of children around circles.

    Teacher chooses two attributes such as shape and color, shape and size or color and size. Children name pieces by shape, size, and color. Pieces with one attribute will be placed in one city. Pieces with the other attribute will be placed in the other city. The intersection is kept clear at this time. Pieces with neither attribute are put aside.

    When all the city pieces have been named, the children describe the attributes for each city (for instance triangles, city one; reds, city 2).

    Guide children to discover that some shapes have attributes of each city. Place these in the intersection.

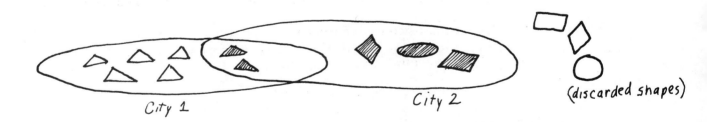

Today we're going to build a city. I'm the city builder. I have a plan for both cities. Try to guess my plan by naming a shape.

If your shape is part of my plan I'll put it in the city where it belongs. If not, I'll put it over here (point). Guess only things that belong in the cities.

Tell me about this city (point to one of cities). How are the shapes alike? Tell me about the other city.

Are there any shapes which belong in the intersection? Why?

KEYS TO THE CITY

Objectives   *To show the relationship between two groups of objects by using two intersecting circles (Venn diagram).*

*To use the word **and** to describe the attributes of the objects in the intersection of the two circles.*

Preparation   *Use worksheets 1 and 2. Color as directed. Cut out shapes and place on floor (stack #1). Cut out cards from worksheet 17 and place face down in another stack (stack #2).*

Use two colors of yard or plastic hoops. Place on floor to form two overlapping circles.

Choose two children to play the game. Each child picks a card from stack #2 and looks at it. Each places card face down at the edge of own city under yarn or hoop. This card is the attribute to be used for making child's city.

Children take turns picking a shape from stack #1, asking if it belongs in opponent's city. Children try to guess what is written on the opponent's card. The first one to guess correctly wins.

Cards can be reshuffled and the game can be played again.

Each person pick a card and look at it. Put it face down under the edge of your city. This is the key to your city. It tells what goes in your city. You are going to try to guess what your opponent's key is as soon as possible.

Take turns picking shapes. Say to your opponent, "This shape belongs/does not belong in my city; does it belong in yours?"

If it belongs to your opponent, place the shape in your opponent's city. If it belongs to you, place it in your city. If it belongs to both cities, place the shape in the intersection. If it belongs to neither city, place it away from the city.

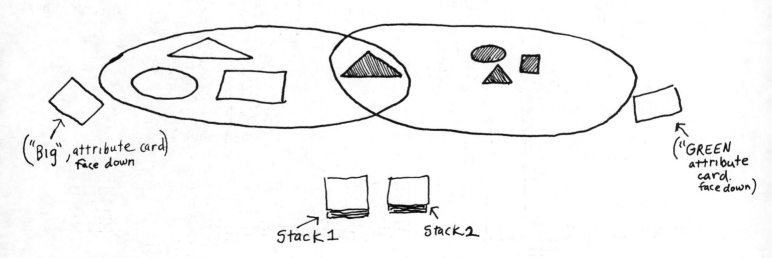

("Big", attribute card)
face down

("GREEN attribute card. face down)

Stack 1   Stack 2

OTHER GAMES AND ACTIVITIES FOR LEVEL 6

The following games and activities from Part II can be used with this level:

BEAD GAME #6

VENN DIAGRAM GAME

CARS

WHAT SHALL I WEAR?

MISCELLANEOUS CLASSIFICATION IDEAS

FLYING

THE MARKET

PART II

Multi-Level Activities
for Classification *

*These activities may be done concurrently with the
DEVELOPMENTAL ACTIVITIES in Part I.

LEVEL CHART

Activity	LEVEL					
	1	2	3	4	5	6
Bead Game 1	X					
Bead Game 2		X				
Bead Game 3			X			
Bead Game 4				X		
Bead Game 5					X	
Bead Game 6						X
Venn Diagram Game						X
Gathering Stones	X				X	
Nature Walk	X				X	
Cars	X	X	X	X	X	X
What Shall I Wear?					X	X
TV Time	X				X	
Miscellaneous Classification Ideas	X	X	X	X	X	X
Flying	X	X			X	X
Person Game	X		X			
Murals	X				X	
Practical Application: Daily Living	X				X	
Practical Application: School	X				X	
Practical Application: Library	X				X	
Where To Find It	X				X	
People, Places, Things	X				X	
Pick and Sort	X	X			X	
Concentration	X	X			X	
Sourpuss	X	X			X	
What Color?	X				X	
The Market	X	X	X	X	X	X

BEAD GAME I

Objective   *To sort beads by color or shape*

Preparation   *Give child set of beads and a string for the beads. Direct child to string one kind of bead on the string.*

Make a necklace of all the red beads.

Make a necklace of all the green beads.

Make a necklace of all the yellow beads.

Make a necklace of all the blue beads.

Make a necklace of all the round beads.

Make a necklace of all the square beads.

BEAD GAME 2

Objective   *To sort beads by two attributes as color and shape.*

Preparation   *Give child a set of beads and a string for the beads. Direct child to string beads by giving two attributes.*

Make a necklace of all the red round beads.

Make a necklace of all the yellow square beads.

Use blue cubes to make a necklace.

Make a necklace of the round green beads.

BEAD GAME 3

Objective   *To sort beads by negative attributes*

Preparation *Give child set of beads and a string for the beads. Direct child to string beads by giving negative clues. Child can describe necklace made after clue is given.*

Make a necklace of all the not red beads. Tell me about the necklace.

Make a necklace of all the not yellow beads. Tell me about the necklace.

Make a necklace of all the not green beads. Tell me about the necklace.

Make a necklace of all the not blue beads. Tell me about the necklace.

Make a necklace of all the not round beads. Tell me about the necklace.

Make a necklace of all the not square beads. Tell me about the necklace.

BEAD GAME 4

Objective   *To recognize that a bead can belong to two groups simultaneously.*

Preparation *Give child set of beads and a string for the beads. Direct child to string beads of one color or one shape. Ask quantative questions about the necklaces.*

String all the square beads on the necklace. Are there more red beads or more square beads? Why? Are the red beads square?

Are there more yellow beads or more square beads? Why?

Are there more green beads or more square beads? Why?

Are there more blue beads or more square beads? Why?

Make a necklace of all of the blue beads. Are there more blue beads or more square beads? Why? Are the square beads blue? Or are there some other color square beads on the necklace too?

Are there more blue beads or more round beads? Why?

String all the round beads on the necklace. Are there more red beads or more round beads? Why? Are the round beads all red? Or are there other colors of round beads?

Are there more yellow beads or more round beads? Why?

Are there more green beads or more round beads? Why?

Make a necklace of all of the green beads. Are there more green beads or more square beads? Why?

Are there more green beads or more round beads? Why?

Make a necklace of all the red beads. Are there more red beads or more square beads? Why?

Are there more red beads or more round beads? Why?

Make a necklace of all the yellow beads. Are there more yellow beads or more square beads? Why?

Are there more yellow beads or more round beads? Why?

BEAD GAME 5

Objective   *To define a string of beads by one attribute.*

Preparation *Give child a string on which beads with one attribute (color or shape) have been strung. Example: give child a necklace of all blue beads. Repeat for each color and shape.*

Tell me what is the same about the beads on this necklace. Why do these beads go on this necklace?

BEAD GAME 6

Objective   *To define a set of beads on a string by two attributes.*

Preparation *Give child a string on which beads of one color and shape have been strung. Example: string red round beads on the string. Repeat: red square; yellow round; yellow square; green round; green square; blue round; blue square.*

Tell me what is the same about the beads on this necklace. Why do they belong on the same necklace?

VENN DIAGRAM GAME

Objectives   *To show the relationship between two groups of objects by using two intersecting circles (Venn diagram).*

To use the word and *to describe the attributes of the objects in the intersection of the two circles.*

Preparation   *Prepare two intersecting circles on floor or on a chart or the board. Choose an attribute for each circle and place one picture containing that attribute in each circle.*

Have children cut out magazine pictures that have the attributes chosen. Arrange the pictures in the circles.

After the pictures are arranged in the proper circles, guide the children to see if any of the pictures have the attributes of both circles. Pictures of objects having both attributes are placed in the intersection.

Look for a picture in the magazine that can fit in this circle or in this circle. Cut it out and place it on the circle.

Let's look at the pictures. Why does this picture fit in this circle? (repeat for all pictures in each circle)

Are there any pictures that could fit in either circle? Why? Put those pictures in the intersection.

GATHERING STONES

Objective   *To sort stones by attributes.*

Preparation   *Children bring a stone or small rock to school. The rocks or stones can be sorted in large or small groups by color, shape, texture or . . . .*

Children can later write or tell about how the rocks and stones were sorted.

How can we sort these stones?

Is there another way to sort the stones?

NATURE WALK

Objective   *To sort things seen in nature.*

Preparation   *Discuss ways that things in nature might be sorted. Some categories might include animals, plants, birds, crawling things, furry things, things that are green, things that are not green, etc.*

Take class for a walk.

Children take turns naming an object seen, and the rest of the class names the category to which the object belongs.

Vary the game by having children choose partners. Partners take turns naming objects while the other partner names the category.

On our walk today we are going to classify or sort things we see according to the categories we have talked about. Remember our categories.

When we get back we will draw a picture of some of the things which belong to one of the categories.

CARS

Objectives   *To sort vehicles into groups and define each group by its attribute.*

                     To show that an object might belong to two groups simultaneously.

                     To define objects by negative attributes.

                     To use the terms some *and* all *in defining groups.*

Preparation   *Children cut out a four-wheel, motorized vehicle from a magazine.*

                     Sort the vehicles in some way (color, type of car, number of doors, size, function, etc.)

                     Vehicles can be displayed in one of several ways: simple classification headings, with vehicles glued in proper columns; use of Venn diagrams (to show that vehicle can belong to two groups simultaneously).

                     Teacher can encourage children to discuss the vehicles in negative terms. The teacher can also discuss some *and* all *when talking about the classification.*

How can you sort the cars? Sort them in some way. Tell me how you sorted the vehicles.

Are there some vehicles that belong to two groups at the same time? If we use a Venn diagram to show this, what would go in the intersection?

Show me a group of trucks and a group of not trucks.

Put all of the cars here. Are there more cars or more vehicles?

WHAT SHALL I WEAR?

Objective   *To show how classification skills are used to determine what clothes to wear.*

Preparation   *Seat children for a discussion.*

                         Discuss ways to decide what to wear. What to wear is determined by the weather, by color, by function, by the way you feel.

Why did you decide to wear what you're wearing today?

How do you dress if it is cold?

If it is hot, how do you dress?

If you decide to wear a red shirt, how do you decide what color pants or skirt to wear?

What things do you wear in the rain?

If you were going to a party, what would you wear? Would you dress differently to go to school?

56

TV TIME

Objective   *To classify TV programs by content.*

Preparation   *Have children list favorite TV programs on board or chart. Teacher should be aware of the content of programs.*

Have children suggest categories for classifying the programs.

Name your favorite TV programs.

Are there two programs that are alike in some way? How are they alike?

Are there other programs that are like those?

Let's classify the programs and organize them so that we put like programs together.

Categories   *Sports, police stories, news, cowboys, cartoons*

MISCELLANEOUS CLASSIFICATION IDEAS

Objectives   *To name objects that belong in a group.*

To subdivide the group into smaller groups.

To discuss the groups in negative terms.

To use the terms some *and* all *in describing groups.*

Preparation   *Have children determine classification category or tell them the category.*

Have children name objects which would fit in the category. List things on a chart or on the board.

Have children subdivide list.

Suggestions   Things we use at school, things we don't use at school.

Things that fly, things that swim, things that crawl.

Things we use for work, things we use for play.

Things we find in the kitchen, things we find in the living room.

Things that sink, things that float.

Things a magnet will attract, things a magnet won't attract.

58

FLYING

Objectives   *To name objects that can fly.*

To show that this class of objects can be subdivided into smaller groups.

Preparation   *Have children name things that can fly.*

List things on a chart or on the board.

Have children subdivide this list into categories, i.e., things alive/things not alive; things that have wheels/things not having wheels; things that have motors/things not having motors, etc.

What are some things that you can think of that can fly?

Let's find a way to organize or classify them. Are there two things on the list that are alike in some way? How are they alike? Does anything else from the list fit into that group?

How else could we group the things that fly?

THE PERSON GAME

Objective   *To choose a person from negative clues.*

Preparation   *Seat children so they can see each other. Teacher chooses a child to describe using the word* not. *Class tries to guess who the teacher is thinking about. Teacher responds by giving more negative clues.*

The child who guesses correctly can think of the next person to give negative clues about.

I'm thinking of someone in the room. It is *not* Susie.

Class: Is it Mary?

It is *not* Mary. I'm thinking of someone who is *not* a girl.

Class: Is it Jimmy?

It is *not* Jimmy. I'm thinking of someone who is *not* wearing blue.

MURALS

Objective

To use art to reinforce the concept that objects can be sorted into groups by attributes.

Preparation

Cut a large piece of butcher paper or chart paper. Place this in an area which will accommodate several children. Put out proper materials as crayons or paint, scissors, glue, magazines.

Suggested
Themes

GROCERY STORE: Color and label sections of the grocery store.

ANIMALS: Cut pictures out of newspapers, magazines or books, or draw animals appropriate to the categories written on the paper. Categories may be determined by the teacher or by the class. Some categories might include: farm animals, domestic animals (pets), jungle animals, zoo animals, circus animals.

COLORS: Cut out different colors of objects from magazines and glue them in the appropriate spaces on the paper. The teacher will have color words written on the paper.

SHAPES: Cut pictures out of magazines or draw shapes appropriate to the categories written on the paper. Categories may be determined by the teacher or by the class and might include: Rounds (balls, balloons, saucers, wheels), Squares (boxes, houses, squares in tennis nets, window panes, sidewalk), Triangles (tops of churches, roofs, window panes, dome section), Rectangles (houses, window panes, doors, sidewalks), Cylinders (silo, cigarette, salt shaker).

PRACTICAL APPLICATION: DAILY LIVING

Objectives *To show how classification is used in every day life.*

To show that organization or classification gives order to living.

Preparation *Seat children for a discussion.*

Classifying things or organizing makes life easier. It makes things more simple to do. At your house you put your clothes in a closet and you put the kitchen utensils in the kitchen. Why do you do this?

Can you find things easier if you know where they might be?

If you wanted to use the potato masher, where would you look?

If you needed a towel to dry yourself, where would you look?

Where would you most likely find your tennis shoes?

Look in the kitchen drawers tonight at home and find out how Mother organizes her drawers. Color a picture of one of the drawers. (Children might find utensils sorted by function, i.e., all spoons, all knives, all forks, big plates, little plates, etc.)

How could you sort your clothes in the closet? Can you put all your shirts or blouses together? Could you put all of your blue blouses together? Or could you put all of your red clothes together? Go home tonight and ask your mother if you can organize your closet in some way. Color a picture to show how you organized your closet. Bring it to school.

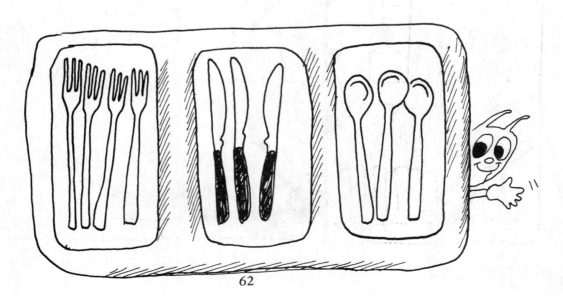

PRACTICAL APPLICATION: SCHOOL

Objectives   *To show how classification is used at school.*

To show that classification at school makes it easier for everyone to find things.

Preparation   *Seat children for a discussion. Have children practice classification during school day.*

When we organize or classify things at school, it is easier for everyone to find things. If you wanted to read a book, where would you go to look for one?

Is it easier to think about looking for a book in the book case than to think about looking for a book in the coat closet? Do we organize other things in the room?

Can we sort the books on the shelf in some way? (type of book, size, color)

Name some ways to organize games on the game shelf. (size, color, function as math game, reading games)

Sort the crayons in some way. (color, length)

63

PRACTICAL APPLICATION: LIBRARY LESSON

Objective   *To show how classification of books in the library makes it easier to find books.*

Preparation   *Take the children to the library. Discuss how the library is organized. (picture books, fiction books, non-fiction books, etc.)*

Find an easy or picture book.

Where would you look for a book about animals?

Find a book about poems.

What other things are there to read in a library? Where are they kept?

Find a book written by an author whose name begins with M.

WHERE TO FIND IT

Objective   *To show how organization and classification are used in everyday life.*

To show that certain things are found in certain stores.

Preparation   *Seat children for a discussion.*

Each child thinks of something to buy. Children take turns naming what they are going to buy. The rest of the class must name the store where the object can be bought.

I'm looking for a place to buy some clothes. Where shall I go? (department store)

I'm looking for a place to have my clothes cleaned. Where shall I go? (cleaners)

Other situations:
   Buy shoes, buy medicine, buy oil for the car, wash clothes, get an ice cream cone, etc.

PEOPLE, PLACES, THINGS

Objective   *To classify pictures according to the categories: people, places, or things.*

Preparation   *Use worksheet 21. Prepare spinner by cutting on lines and mounting on a piece of stiff paper or cardboard cut to the size of the spinner. Use a thin stick or a piece of cardboard cut in shape of arrow.*
Punch a hole in arrow. Attach arrow to spinner with a paper brad. Use washer between spinner and arrow.

Use worksheet 23 to prepare game board for each player. Give each player (2 or 3) one token.

Players take turns spinning the spinner and moving own token to the next picture that matches the classification spun.

The first player to reach the center of the board wins the game.

Spin the spinner and read the category. Move your token to the next picture which belongs to that category. The first person to reach the center of the board is the winner.

PICK AND SORT

Objective   *To sort objects into categories.*

Preparation   *Use Worksheet 24 to prepare a deck of cards. Cut along the lines. Shuffle and place face down on floor or table.*

Use Worksheet 23 to prepare a game board for each player.

Players take turns picking a card. The card is placed on the game board in the proper category. If there is no room for the card, it is placed in the discard pile.

When no cards are left in the drawing pile, shuffle the discard pile and use it as the drawing pile.

The first player to fill one category wins the game.

Vary the game by playing until the game board is filled.

Take turns picking a card from the drawing pile. Look at the picture and put it on your game board in the right category. The first person to fill one row or category is the winner.

CONCENTRATION

Objective   *To recognize that certain objects belong to the same category or classification*

Preparation   *Use Worksheets 18, 19, and 20. Prepare a deck of cards by cutting on the line. Remove the "Sourpuss" card.*

Spread the cards face down on the floor or on a table.

Players take turns picking up two cards. If the two cards picked belong to the same category, the cards are put together in a book and placed face down in the book pile. The player gets another turn.

If the cards don't belong to the same category, the cards are turned over. The next player takes a turn.

The player with the most books at the end of the game is the winner.

Take turns picking two cards. If the cards belong to the same category, put them together in a book and place them face down in a book pile. Then take another turn. Each time you make a book you get another turn.

If the cards do not match, turn them face down and it is time for the other player's turn.

The player with the most books at the end of the game is the winner.

SOURPUSS

Objective
: *To recognize that certain objects belong to the same category or classification.*

Preparation
: *Use Worksheets 18, 19 and 20. Prepare a deck of cards by cutting on the line. Shuffle and deal five cards to each of two players. Place remaining cards face down between the players.*

  Players pick up cards dealt and hold in hand. If a player is holding two cards that belong to the same category, these two cards can be put together in a book. The book is placed face down on the player's book pile.

  Players take turns picking one card from opponent's hand and trying to make a book by matching card picked to a card in own hand. The dealer gets the first turn.

  Each time a book is made, it is placed face down in the book pile and the player draws a new card from the draw pile.

  When the draw pile is gone, players continue picking cards from each other's hands until all the cards are made into books. The player holding "Sourpuss" is the loser.

Deal each person five cards. Pick up your cards and look at them. See if you have any cards that belong to the same group. You might have two tools or two people or two vegetables. If you can match two cards belonging to the same group, put them together in a book. Put the book down in front of you and take a card from the draw pile.

Now take turns drawing a card from your opponent's hand. Try to make a book using that card and one from your own hand. If you do, put it face down and take one card from the draw pile.

Someone has a "Sourpuss" card. Whoever is left with that card at the end of the game is the loser.

WHAT COLOR?

Objectives   *To recognize that certain objects have a given color.*

                 To determine what color objects should be.

                 To sort pictures of the objects by color.

Preparation   *Use worksheet 25. Color as directed. Cut cards on line and place on floor or chalk ledge.*

                 Prepare worksheet 26 by cutting on lines. Have children sit so they can see color cards. Discuss colors of objects.

                 Have children match non-colored pictures to appropriate color.

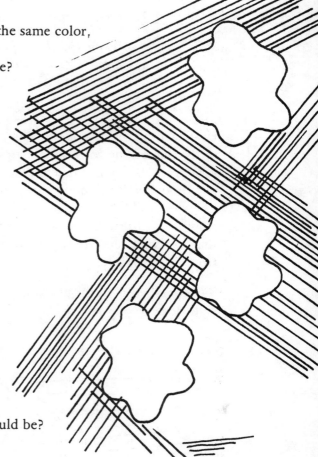

Some things that we see around us are always the same color,

What color is a banana? Is it ever orange or blue?

Tell me some things that are always red.

Tell me some things that are always orange.

Tell me some things that are always yellow.

Tell me some things that are always green.

Tell me some things that are always blue.

Tell me some things that are always purple.

Tell me some things that are always brown.

Tell me some things that are always black.

Tell me some things are are always white.

Can you match your picture to the color it should be?

Extension:
Give each child a copy of worksheet 26 to color appropriately.
Play concentration with the set of colors and one set of outlined pictures. Turn cards face down.
Children take turns drawing 2 cards.
If the picture matches the color, the child gets one more turn.
Child with the most cards wins.

THE MARKET

As an on-going activity, "The Market" could be started early in the classification unit and continue throughout all six levels. When used in this way, dramatic play and concepts would increase in complexity as more advanced levels are reached.

An alternative is to use "The Market" as a multi-level culmination at the end of the classification unit.

INTRODUCTION

Read the following poem to the class.

WHAT DO YOU THINK I BOUGHT?

I went to the store
With a bright new nickel.
What do you think I bought?
A big dill pickle!

I went to the store
With a shiny dime.
What do you think I bought?
A big, green lime.

I went to the store
With half a dollar.
What do you think I bought?
Some soap for my collar.

I went to the store
With a piece of string.
What do you think I bought?
Not a thing.

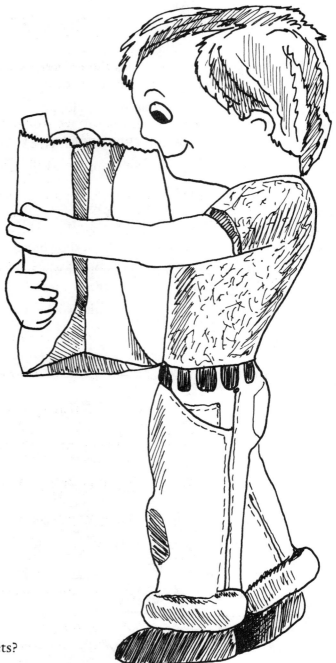

DISCUSSION

What kinds of things do you buy in the market?

Where do you find these products?

What would you find in the produce section?
What would you find in the refrigerator case?
What would you find in the frozen food section?
What would you find in the bakery section?

Name other sections (departments).

Why do we have sections or departments in markets?

ORGANIZING A MARKET: DRAMATIC PLAY

MAKE A MARKET

Either have a market corner or build markets with blocks, draw markets outside or in the room with chalk on the floor.

Cut out pictures of food to use.

PLAY MARKET

Play market by dividing children into groups.

Let one group be the grocers.
This group organizes the groceries and then explains how and why they classified the products as they did. (cans, fruits, vegetables, etc.)

Let another group be the shoppers and "evaluate" the grocers' organization.

TAKING A FIELD TRIP: CREATIVE EXPRESSION

Have everyone take his or her own field trip to the supermarket.

Share experiences.
Tell what each person saw.
Write, draw or paint about it.

Make miniature markets in shoe boxes (dioramas).

Older children make three-dimentional store miniatures.
Put the models on a piece of cardboard.

As a class project, everyone work on a supermarket mural.

CREATIVE EXPRESSION

LANGUAGE ARTS

SHARING EXPERIENCES

Have children tell about experiences or things that are classified by area or similarities. For instance, share vacation experiences, ghost stories, favorite foods, jokes, TV programs, books, etc.

MUSIC: ACTIVITY SONGS

Two excellent sources for using music to learn classification skills are the activity songs "Mix and Match" and "Square Dance." These selections were written to supplement this book and are contained in the album "It's A Happy Feeling" published by Rhythms Productions. The activities in these songs help develop skills in classifying objects by shape, color and size.

MIX AND MATCH

Classifying by shape and size

To prepare for the game, divide group into circles and squares. Divide again into big and little circles and squares. Make signs (or crowns) to wear showing own shape and size.

To play the game, follow the words to the songs. Trade signs for new games so everyone is all shapes and sizes.

SQUARE DANCE

Classifying by shape and color

To prepare for the game, use 1 shape (square) and 4 colors (red, yellow, blue, green). Every person choose a color. Make a square and color it your color. Wear your square and follow the calls.

Calls are invented by the leader (teacher or class). The calls tell red, yellow, green and blue squares to do something. For example:

All squares stand up.	Blue squares stand up.
All squares sit down.	Green squares stand up.
Yellow squares stand up.	Yellow and blue squares sit down.
Red squares stand up.	Red and green squares sit down.

Trade colors and repeat the game. To vary the game, make the calls harder by using more shapes. Use 2 shapes and 2 or 4 colors. Use shape and size instead of shape and color.

GAMES

Many games are based on classifications. For very young children, a simple game like "Stand up if...you are wearing red, have blue eyes," etc.

Games can be more complicated for older children, as in this guessing game. The classification is animals. The player says, "I'm thinking of an animal. The first clue is: The animal is much bigger than I am. What is it?" (Children each get one guess.)

SECOND CLUE: It has sharp claws.
THIRD CLUE: It likes to catch fish.

Clues are given until the animal is guessed. The person who guesses chooses another animal (or classification) and the game begins again.

PART III

TESTING UNIT

FORMAT AND DIRECTIONS

This unit is included for use in situations that are oriented to teaching by objectives. It may also be used to create an individualized learning curriculum.

The components consist of duplicating masters for the following:

TEACHER MATERIALS   Pre- and Post-Test questions
Class Record Forms

STUDENT MATERIALS   Concept Sheets for multiple concepts

The diagram below shows one suggested operational format or sequence for the program:

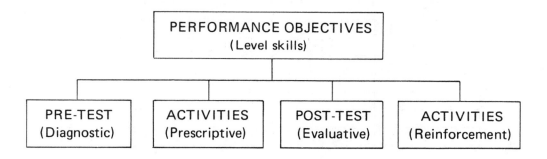

PERFORMANCE OBJECTIVES consist of mastery of the skills in each of the six classification levels.

PRE-TESTS indicate the child's weaknesses and strengths in terms of these skills. (diagnostic)

ACTIVITIES support learning for each developmental level. (prescriptive)

POST-TESTS verify learning by measuring performance of the skills. (evaluative)

ACTIVITIES reinforce learning of skills at levels still not mastered. (prescriptive)

DIRECTIONS FOR USING THE PRE-TEST

Use the Pre-Test to determine the initial amount of concept understanding that each child has.

1. Reproduce Concept Sheets.

2. Use suggested questions and note each child's performance on Class Record Form.

3. If the concept is understood, indicate on the form with a + in the PRE column.

4. If the concept is missed, indicate on the form with a − in the PRE column.

5. Consult the chart for question levels.

QUESTION	LEVELS			
	1	2	3	4
1	X			
2		X		
3		X		
4		X		
5	X			
6	X			
7			X	
8			X	
9				X
10				X
11			X	X
12			X	X

Levels 5 and 6 should be tested by giving children things to sort. Children will show their understanding at this level by sorting objects and telling how they did so.

ACTIVITIES FOR LEARNING

When problems in level areas have been diagnosed, choose appropriate activities from the book to create an individualized learning program.

DIRECTIONS FOR USING THE POST-TEST

Following the activity program, give the Post-Test to determine the extent of learning that has taken place.

1. Reproduce the Concept Sheets.

2. Use the word or words in the parenthesis with the suggested questions.

3. If the concept is understood, indicate on the form with a + in the POST column.

4. If the concept is missed, indicate on the form with a − in the POST column.

5. Consult the chart for question levels.

QUESTION	LEVELS			
	1	2	3	4
1	X			
2		X		
3		X		
4		X		
5	X			
6	X			
7			X	
8			X	
9				X
10				X
11			X	X
12			X	X

REINFORCEMENT

From the results of the Post-Test, repeat activities to reinforce concept learning in areas that are not understood.

Individual instruction or home study may be prescribed to help promote learning in these problem areas.

TEST QUESTIONS

PICTURE KEY   QUESTIONS

Page 1

SUN

1. Put your marker under the row that begins with the sun. Make an X on the shape that belongs to a group of squares. A group of squares. (Make an X on the shape that belongs to a group of diamonds, circles, triangles.)

SPOON

2. Move your marker down to the row that begins with a spoon. Make an X on something that belongs to a group of animals. A group of animals. (Make an X on something that belongs to a group of clothes; a group of clothes).

APPLE

3. Move your marker down to the row that begins with the apple. Make an X on something big and round. Big and round. (Make an X on something small and triangular; small and triangular).

BALLOON

4. Move your marker down to the row that begins with the balloon. Make an X on something that can be big and orange. Big and orange. (Make an X on something that can be little and green, little and green; or big and green; or little and orange).

Page 2

LEAF

5. Go on to the next page. Find the row that begins with the leaf. Make an X on something which rides on four wheels. Something that rides on four wheels. (Make an X on something that can fly; something that can fly).

HOUSE

6. Move your marker down to the row that begins with a house. Make an X on something for work. Something for work. (Make an X on something for play; something for play.

MOUSE

7. Move your marker down to the row that begins with the mouse. Put your marker under the row that begins with the mouse. Make an X on something that is *not* a zoo animal. *Not* a zoo animal. (Make an X on something that does *not* have a tail; does *not* have a tail).

CAR

8. Move your marker down to the row that begins with a car. Make an X on something that is *not* a food. Something that is *not* a food. (Make an X on something that is *not* yellow; something that is *not* yellow).

TEST QUESTIONS

Page 3

FLOWER   9.   Go on to the next page. Find the row that begins with the flower. Make an X where *some* are circles. Make an X where *some* are circles. (Make an X where some are triangles; some are triangles).

KNIFE   10.   Move your marker down to the row that begins with a knife. Make an X where *some* are bees. Make an X where *some* are bees. (Make an X where some are butterflies; some are butterflies).

TURTLE   11.   Move your marker down to the row that begins with a turtle. Make an X where some are not fish. Make an X where some are not fish. (Make an X where some are not birds; make an X where some are not birds).

WAGON   12.   Move your marker down to the row that begins with the wagon. Make an X on something that is *not* a carpenter's tool. *Not* a carpenter's tool. (Make an X on something which is *not* found in a tool kit; something usually *not* found in a tool kit).

"MIX AND MATCH"   **CONCEPT SHEET 1**   © Rhythms Productions

"MIX AND MATCH" CONCEPT SHEET 2 © Rhythms Productions

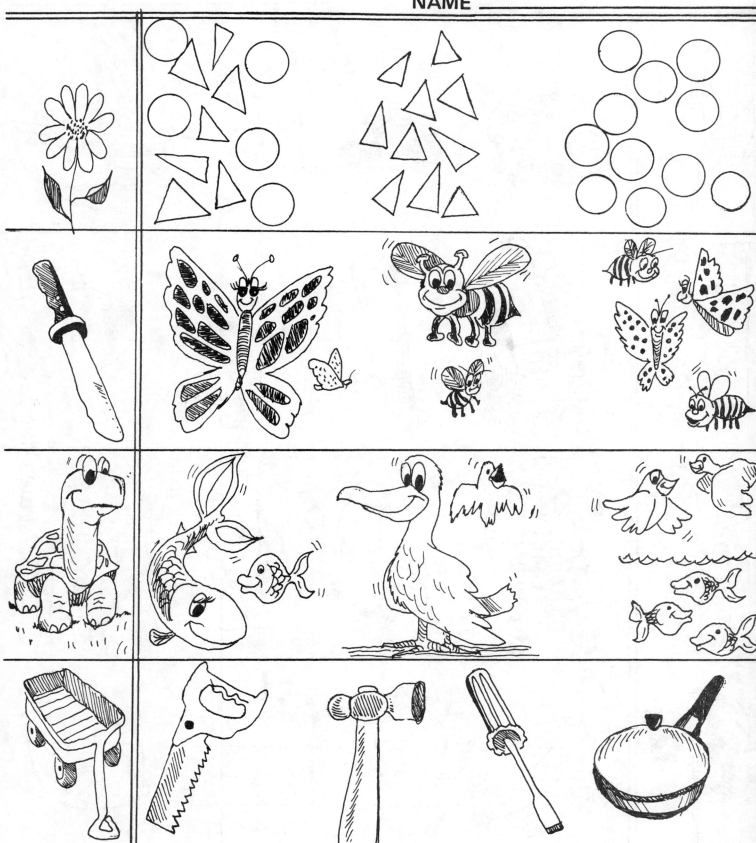

"MIX AND MATCH"   CONCEPT SHEET 3   © Rhythms Productions

CLASS RECORD FORM

NAME	1		2		3		4		5		6		7		8		9		10		11		12	
	Pre	Post	Pre	Post	Pre	Post	Pre	Post	Pre	Post	Pre	Post	Pre	Post	Pre	Post	Pre	Post	Pre	Post	Pre	Post	Pre	Post

QUESTION LEVELS

1 — LEVEL 1	4 — LEVEL 2	7 — LEVEL 3	10 — LEVEL 4
2 — LEVEL 1	5 — LEVEL 1	8 — LEVEL 3	11 — LEVEL 3, 4
3 — LEVEL 2	6 — LEVEL 1	9 — LEVEL 4	12 — LEVEL 3, 4

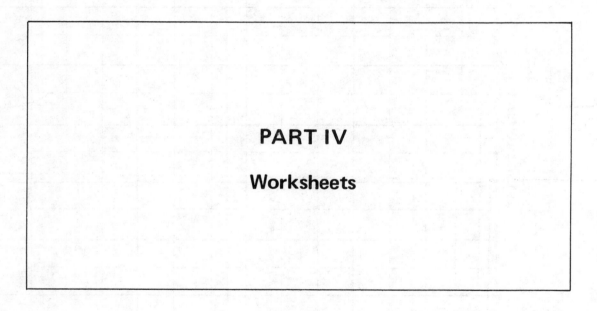

PART IV

Worksheets

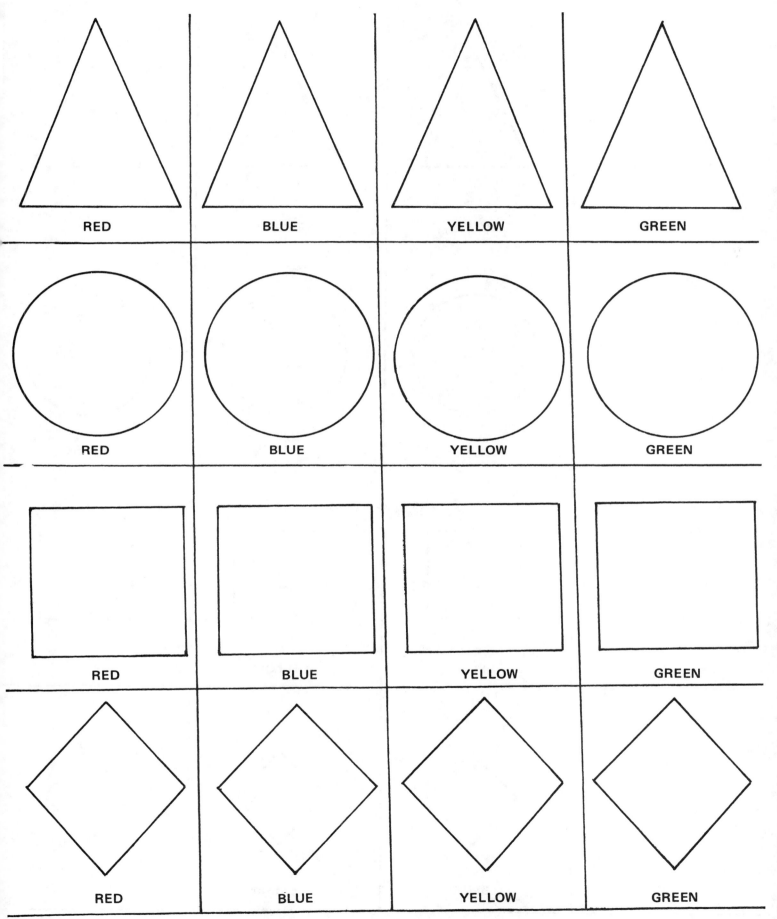

RED	BLUE	YELLOW	GREEN
RED	BLUE	YELLOW	GREEN
RED	BLUE	YELLOW	GREEN
RED	BLUE	YELLOW	GREEN

"MIX AND MATCH"   **Worksheet 1**   © Rhythms Productions

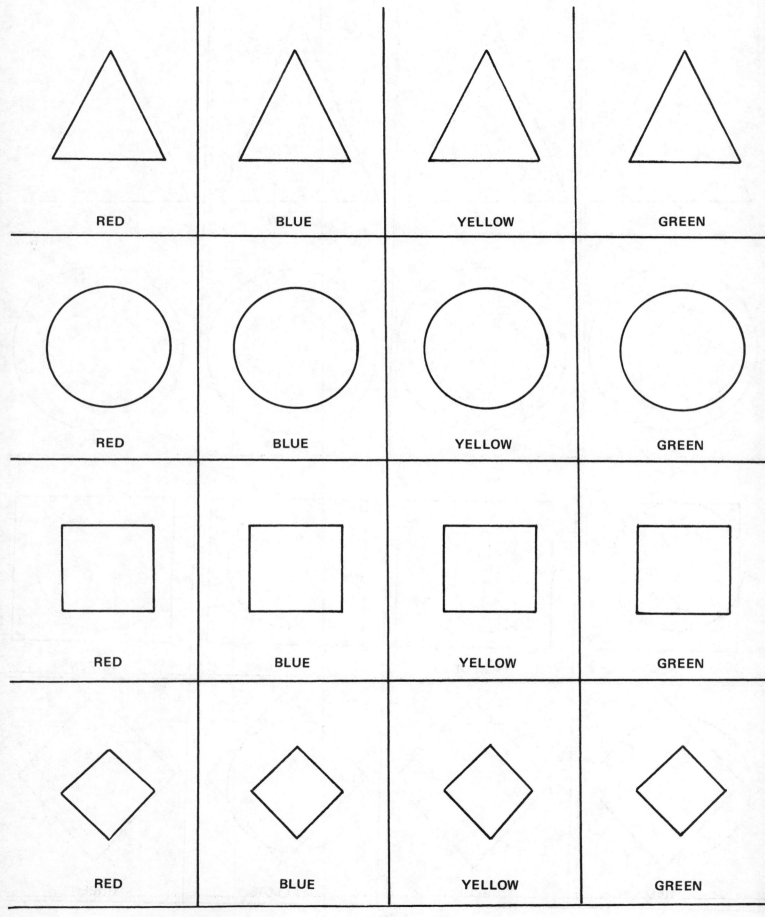

RED   BLUE   YELLOW   GREEN

RED   BLUE   YELLOW   GREEN

RED   BLUE   YELLOW   GREEN

RED   BLUE   YELLOW   GREEN

"MIX AND MATCH"   **Worksheet 2**   © **Rhythms Productions**

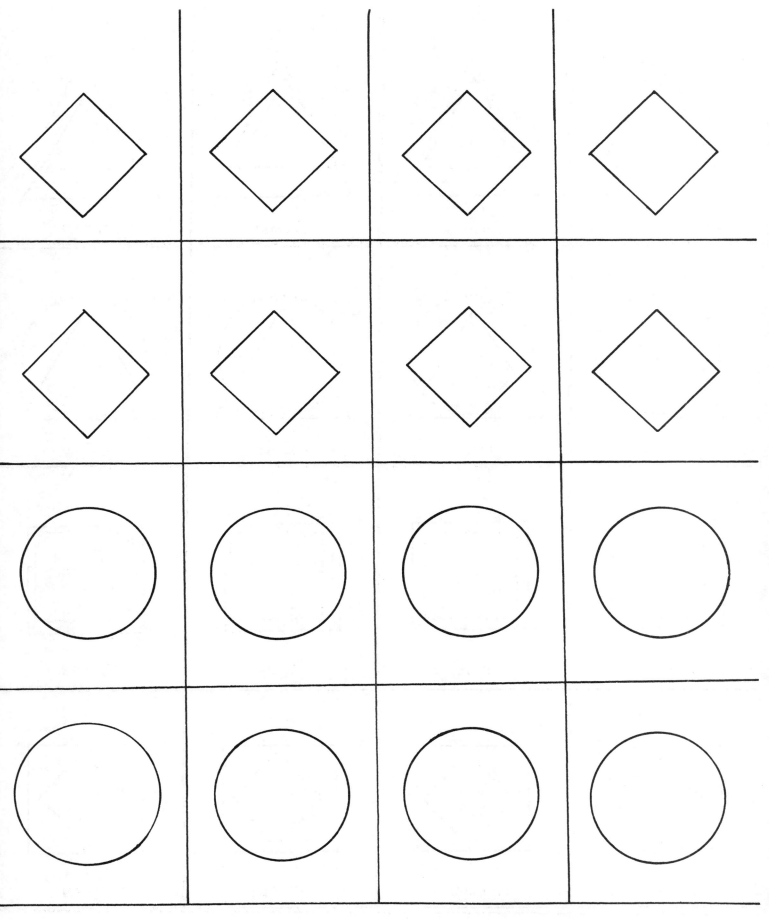

87

"MIX AND MATCH" **Worksheet 4** © Rhythms Productions

"MIX AND MATCH" **Worksheet 5** © Rhythms Productions

"MIX AND MATCH"

"MIX AND MATCH" **Worksheet 8** © Rhythms Productions

"MIX AND MATCH"

© Rhythms Productions

"MIX AND MATCH"

"MIX AND MATCH"

"MIX AND MATCH"   **Worksheet 12**   © Rhythms Productions

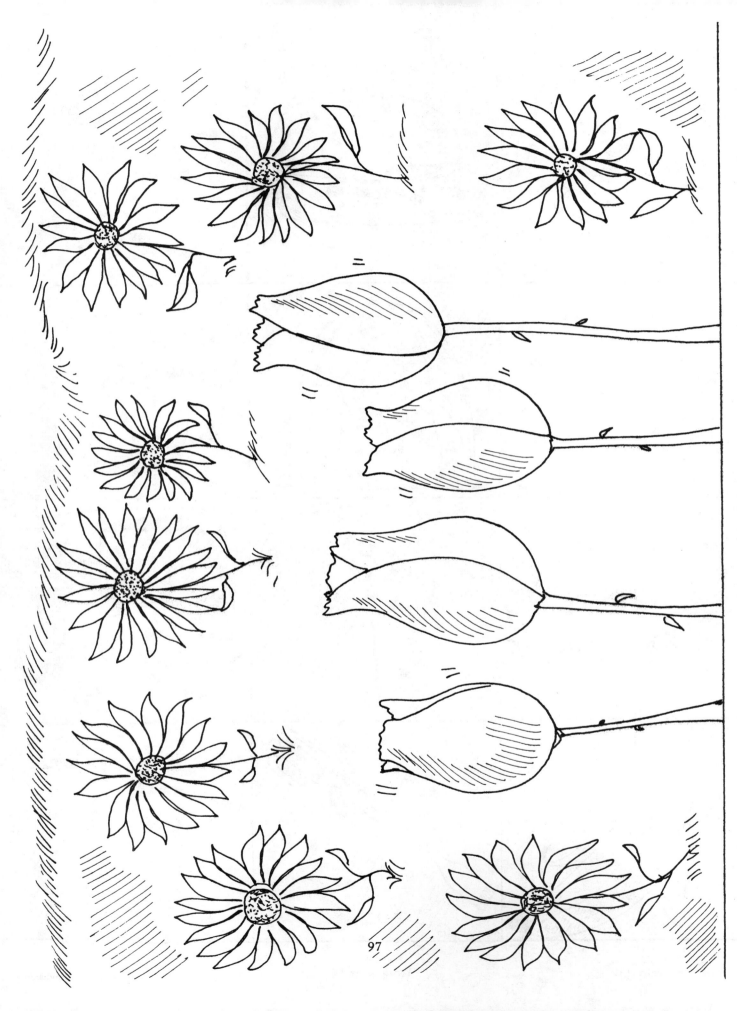

"MIX AND MATCH"

97

"MIX AND MATCH"

"MIX AND MATCH"   **Worksheet 15**   © Rhythms Productions

"SOMETHING" SPINNER GAME

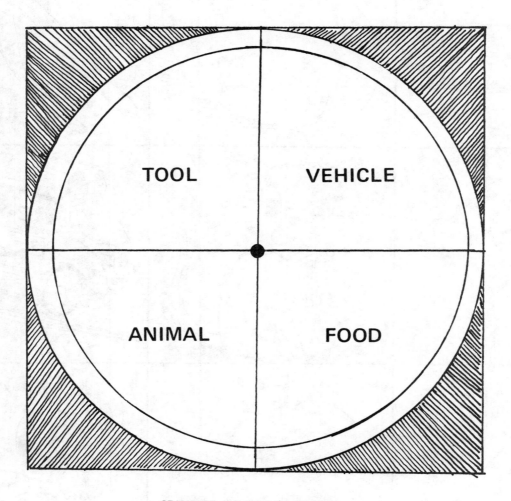

TOOL

VEHICLE

ANIMAL

FOOD

SPINNER BOARD PATTERN

SPINNER ARM PATTERN

RED	LITTLE
YELLOW	⬤
GREEN	⬛
BLUE	◆
BIG	▲

"MIX AND MATCH"

"MIX AND MATCH"

Worksheet 19

© Rhythms Productions

"MIX AND MATCH"

"PEOPLE, PLACES, THINGS" SPINNER GAME

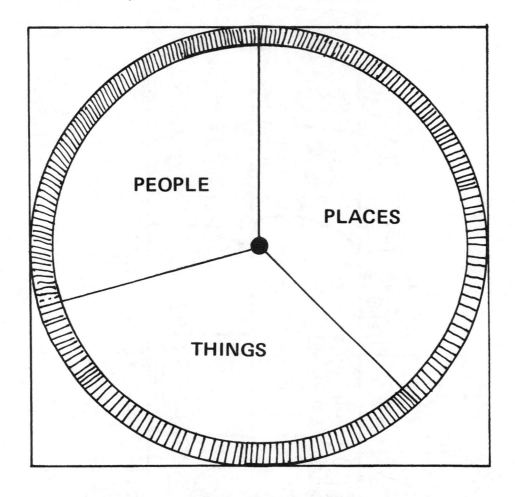

SPINNER BOARD PATTERN

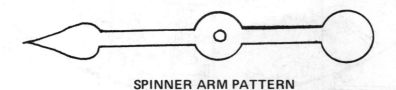

SPINNER ARM PATTERN

"MIX AND MATCH"   © Rhythms Productions

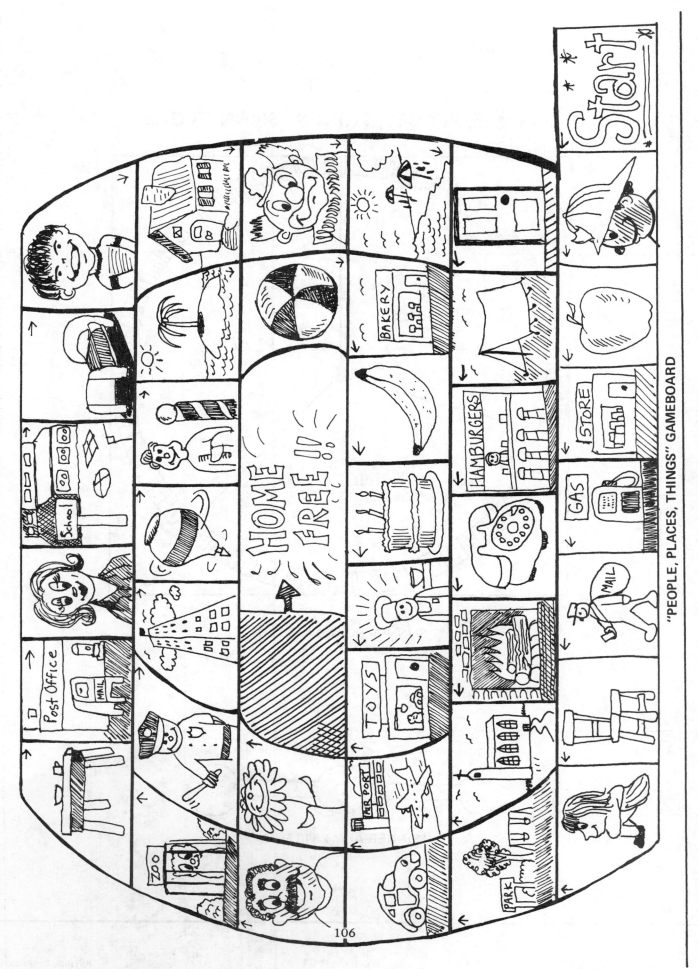

106

"MIX AND MATCH"   "PEOPLE, PLACES, THINGS" GAMEBOARD   Worksheet 22

ANIMAL	ANIMAL	ANIMAL	ANIMAL
FOOD	FOOD	FOOD	FOOD
CLOTHES	CLOTHES	CLOTHES	CLOTHES

"MIX AND MATCH"

Worksheet 23

107

"MIX AND MATCH"   Worksheet 24   © Rhythms Productions

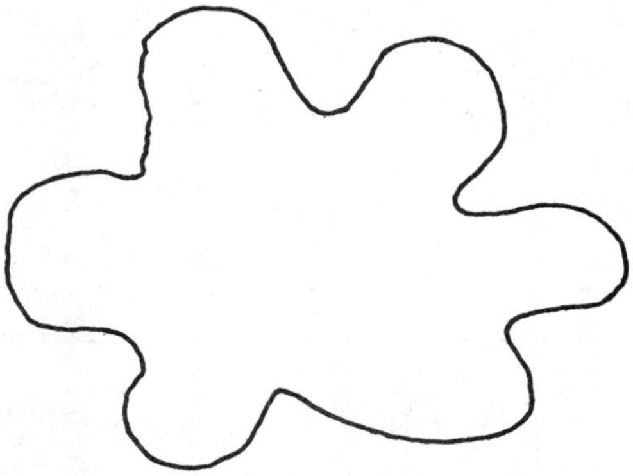

GREEN

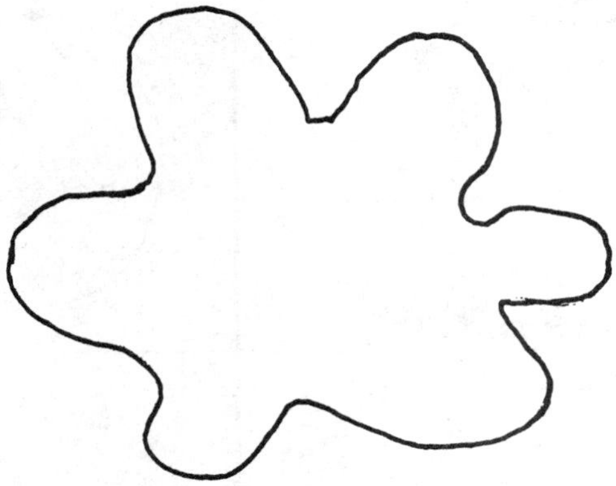

WHITE

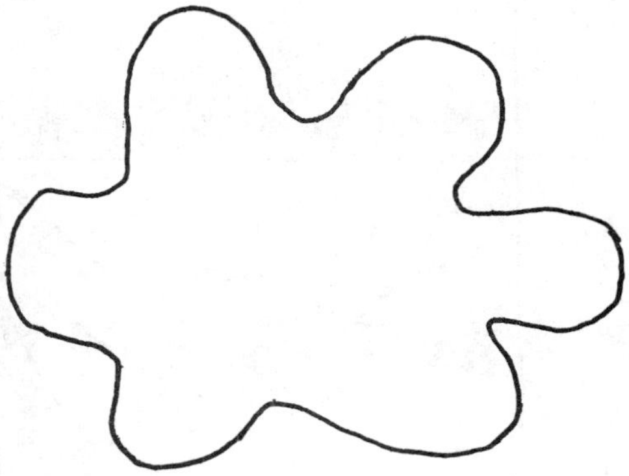

BLUE

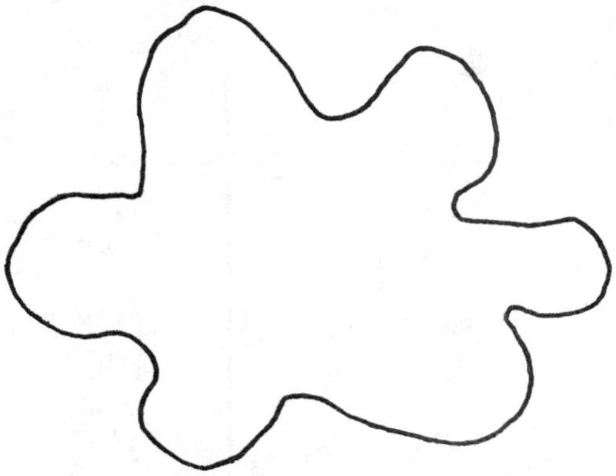

BROWN

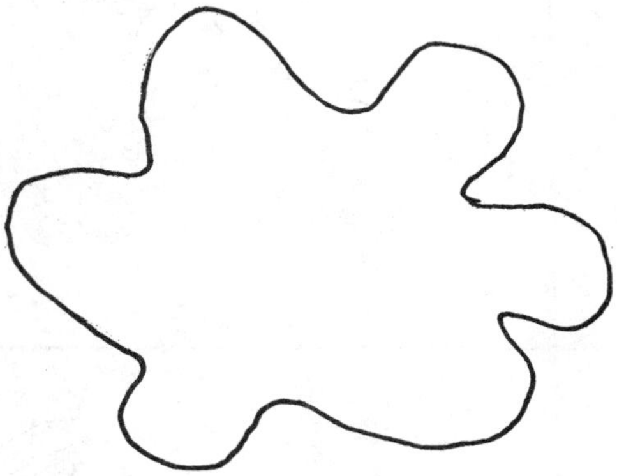

YELLOW

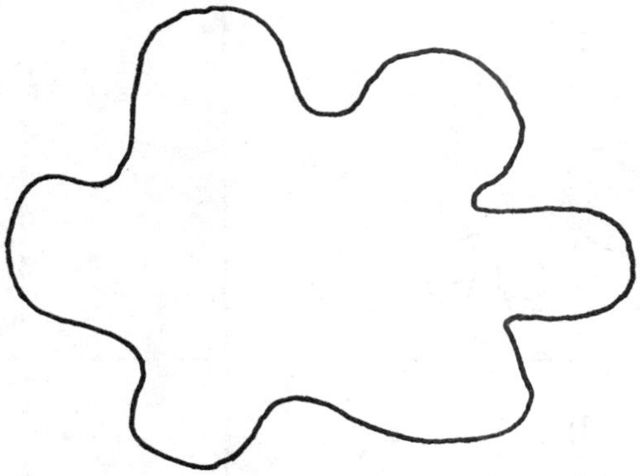

BLACK

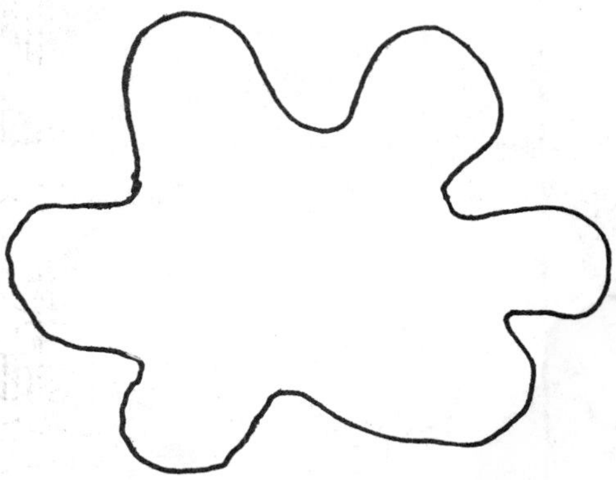

RED

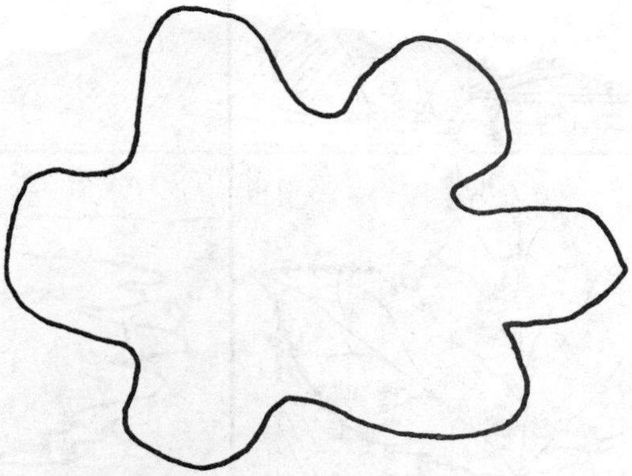

PURPLE

"MIX AND MATCH"   Worksheet 25   © Rhythms Productions

"MIX AND MATCH"   **Worksheet 26**   © Rhythms Productions

NOTES

NOTES